Instrument of Peace

An inspirational book of
healing, comfort and consolation
through the music of the harp

Companion CD Included

Sister Malinda Gerke, FSPA

Dedication

To our loving God, the giver of all good gifts

To the hundreds of people for whom I have played

*They encouraged me in my work by their smiles and kind words.
They have shared their stories with me, and God has blessed
me through them.*

All quotations from Scripture are from the New American Bible
United States Conference of Catholic Bishops
3211 4th Street, N.E., Washington, DC 20017-1194 (202) 541-3000
November 11, 2002 Copyright © by United States Conference of Catholic Bishops

Peace is my gift to you...

John 17:27

To   _____

From _____

Date _____

May this book be a source of consolation and comfort.
May you know God's love and concern for you.
May healing of mind, body and spirit be yours.

Sister Malinda

Acknowledgements

I am grateful to the many persons who have encouraged me and helped in the completion of this book. First and above all, I am grateful to God, who has given me the grace to work in this blessed ministry. I am also grateful to the staff at Gundersen Lutheran - especially Lori Van Lin, Coordinator of Volunteer Services, and to Franciscan Skemp Healthcare - especially Elaine George, Coordinator of Volunteer Services, and to the various nursing homes throughout the area for allowing me to play for their clientele.

My religious community, the Franciscan Sisters of Perpetual Adoration, has been most generous in restoring our antique harp and allowing me to learn to play this wonderful instrument. The community has encouraged me to do my work on a volunteer basis, thus allowing me to make this ministry available to a wider clientele. The writing of this book was under the auspices of the community and would probably not have been completed without the backing of the community leadership team of Sisters Marlene Weisenbeck, Paulynn Instenes, Karen Neuser, Linda Mershon and Sharon Berger.

The communications office of FSPA, headed by Jane Comeau, was instrumental in procuring a publisher and preparing the manuscript. Whitehall Publishing Company has been most encouraging and the staff have been expertly helpful. Bonnie Marlewski-Probert, publisher, and Kristen Spinning, designer, presented us with an outstanding finished product. I am grateful for their expertise.

My gratitude to Donna Gerke-Cuta who created the original art-work. Photographs are the work of Nancy Chapman, Sister Arlene Melder and Kristen Spinning. Gayda Hollnagel and Susan T. Hessel assisted in editing and preparing the book for publication. Sisters Margaret Heil and Maria Friedman helped with proofreading.

I also wish to thank Jeff Cozy, of Bright Ideas Multimedia Co., who recorded and prepared the CD which is included in this book.

I am most grateful to everyone who had any part in my work with the harp or the production of this book. I am confident that their efforts have ensured that *Instrument of Peace* will be a successful testimonial to the mercy and kindness of God.

TABLE OF CONTENTS

Dancing Francis holding Brother Sun,
Viterbo University, La Crosse, Wis.

Prayer of Peace

Lord, make me an instrument of your peace.

Where there is hatred, let me sow love.

Where there is injury, pardon;

Where there is doubt, faith;

Where there is despair, hope;

Where there is darkness, light;

and where there is sadness, joy.

O Divine Master, grant that I may not so

much seek to be consoled as to console;

To be understood, as to understand;

To be loved, as to love;

For it is in giving that we receive.

It is in pardoning that we are pardoned.

And it is in dying that we are born

to eternal life.

Prayer attributed to St. Francis of Assisi

Prologue

From ancient times the harp has been associated with comfort and consolation. Medieval religious art portrays angels, as messengers of God, holding harps. In early Celtic culture, harp music was played for three purposes: to facilitate sleep, to support mourning, and to bring joy.

The harp's properties of resonance, range of pitch and tonal color set up an important relationship between the sound and the recipient's conscious or unconscious being.

The stories in this small tome relate how Sister Malinda, a modern messenger of God, gently enters the world of creaturely existence, communicating empathy and conveying healing energy in times of loving and times of pain. The vignettes remind us how the rhythms and tonal magnitudes of the universe are one with our being. When we are free enough to experience this, then we know that our vocation often chooses us. Sister Malinda's testimony confirms this. We observe how her musical presence connects the prose and the passions of life, soothing its most difficult moments and providing epiphanies for the imagination. She possesses an ardor for wholeness that beckons one toward the divine that is at the center of all being.

A mysterious struggle penetrates all of life and art. Henry James candidly describes how this is for those on the path of the sacred.

*We work in the dark - we do what we can -
we give what we have. Our doubt is our
passion, and our passion is our task.*

Sister Malinda has become what she passionately desires - to be an instrument of peace. The loving sound of her harp is inextricably united with the loving presence of her being. Her ego moves aside as she holds the spiritual realm of others in a holy kindness. She has come to know that each person has their resonant tone and their own rhythm, their own cradle of sound which opens into healing and union with one's Creator. Her ministry with the harp reaches the deepest places in the soul.

Sister Marlene Weisenbeck
President
Franciscan Sisters of Perpetual Adoration

Author's Introduction

The stories in this book are true and touch all of us in many ways. I hope my readers will not see them as just my stories but as a suggestion for possibilities in their own lives. The truth is that we can all become instruments of peace or comfort or healing.

God has given each of us unique gifts or "talents." Our task is to identify these gifts and then carve out our ministry in life. Each of us can then be an instrument of peace through whatever way we touch people, be it spiritually, physically, psychologically, emotionally, financially, or in any other way. It could be teaching children to draw, assisting a single mother to manage her finances better, helping in hospice or Habitat for Humanity, or maybe bringing a pet to comfort the aging. The joy such encounters give will not stop with the first recipient but will spill over into the lives of countless others—families, friends, neighbors, work associates, or maybe just chance contacts.

It is never too late to start. My experiences with the harp came later in my life but they have opened to me a whole new world of ordinary miracles and simple joys. I have learned from them to expect God's hand in the ordinary events of life.

My prayer for each of you is that you come to know through personal experience that you can touch the lives of others and bring to them peace and comfort, joy and understanding. The blessing is that these emotions are very contagious. We cannot give them to others without being exposed to them ourselves in a very personal and powerful way.

May each of us be an "instrument of peace."

Sister Malinda Gerke, FSPA

The DIVINE MUSIC of HOPE LIGHTS UP our LIVES

Healing

The **Lord is my Shepherd,** I shall not want;
in verdant pastures He gives me repose;
beside restful waters He leads me;
He refreshes my **soul.**

Psalm 23

Grace

As I entered the room in intensive care, I saw a tiny, white-haired woman propped up in bed. The usual hospital monitors were making small noises. I was so intent on what I was about to do, that I did not notice anyone in the room other than the nurses. I was not told the patient's name, only that she had been in a coma for an extended time.

"Lord, make me an instrument ...." I prayed and then began to play "Amazing Grace, how sweet the sound ...." I continued to play softly for seven or eight minutes. Then I left, taking my harp with me. A nurse followed me, and said, "Do you realize that her blood pressure went down and her oxygen intake went up?" I knew that music helps with things like that, so I wasn't unduly surprised.

"Are you permitted to tell me her name?" I asked tentatively. There are many rules about privacy in hospitals.

"Her name is Grace." The nurse smiled. Then I started to realize that someone else was in control of this whole situation. How did I know that "Amazing Grace" could be so important to this lovely woman?

The nurses told me later that after I left the hospital, Grace's husband entered the room. Grace opened her eyes, looked lovingly at him and asked, "Where am I? Am I in heaven?"

"Well, no, you're in the hospital," the astonished husband stammered.

Grace had spoken her first words since falling into the coma.

After some time in recuperation, Grace was discharged from the hospital and moved with her husband into one of the assisted living homes in the city.

Several months later I was invited to play for the residents at this home during their noon lunch hour. As I entered the dining room, a radiant little lady said to me, "Come here! You are my healing angel! You played my song for me and I had to come back!"

I went over to her and gave her a hug. Although I rejoiced with her at her recovery, I have to admit that I didn't believe that I had anything to do with her coming out of a coma! So much for realizing the actions of God!

Several weeks passed and I had almost forgotten the incident until one of our sisters stopped me in the chapel of our convent and said, "What is this I hear from the nurses at the hospital that you call people out of comas?" It was then I began to realize that God was working through me! It was a very humbling experience. This was one of the first—and is still one of the most dramatic—examples of Divine intervention I have experienced.

Later, when I was invited to have lunch with the residents, I sat at a table with Grace. I asked her if she had undergone a "near-death" experience.

"Oh, yes!" was her immediate reply. "I saw the light and was in such a peaceful place. Then you came and played my song, and I had to come back!"

"Are you sorry?"

"No, my husband was still here, and I love him very much!"

Every month, when I go to the nursing home, I see Grace at the table and I play "Amazing Grace" for her. Her radiant smile is all the thanks I need.

Amazing Grace, how sweet the sound…
'Twas grace that taught my heart to fear, and grace my fears relieved.
How precious did that grace appear, the hour I first believed.
From "Amazing Grace" by John Newton

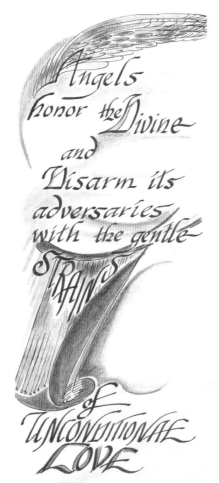

Angels honor the Divine and Disarm its adversaries with the gentle STRAINS of UNCONDITIONAL LOVE

If you order it,

we will look for a person skilled in

playing the harp.

When the pain comes over you,

he will play and you will feel better.

Whenever *the spirit from God* seized Saul,

David would take the harp and play,

and Saul would feel better and be all right again.

Paraphrased from 1 Samuel 16:16-23

Kristie

"Can I help you?" A nurse was standing at my shoulder. As I looked up, I noticed that she was talking to someone on her cell phone.

"Have you ever played in the ICU at Franciscan Skemp Healthcare?" The nurse had placed her hand over the phone.

"Yes, many times. Why do you ask?" The nurse was busy talking to the person on the phone.

"I think this is your lady! Listen!"

The nurse held the phone close to the harp as I continued to play. I could hear Kristie as she said, "Yes, that sounds just like what I heard in the hospital!"

The nurse said good-bye to her friend, then closed her phone and faced me. She told me that Kristie had been suffering from an abnormality of the brain. I had been asked to play for her while she was in the ICU. The doctors did not know what they could do for her. She must have been in the unit for more than a week, because I was asked to play for her more than once. When I was not in the unit, the nursing staff played one of my CDs for Kristie.

Yes, miracles happen. The abnormality is now gone. The doctors can not explain what happened. I have not met Kristie, but I thank God for the intervention that happened and for her improved health.

> *Precious Lord, take my hand, lead me on, let me stand;*
> *I am tired, I am weak, I am worn.*
> *Through the storm, through the night, lead me on to the light....*
> *From "Precious Lord" by Thomas A. Dorsey*

Everyone take heed, all the world listen,

high and low, rich and poor alike:

I have **wisdom** you need to hear.

I see to the heart of things.

I tune my ear to **the truth** and set my

insight to **music.**

Psalm 49:1-5

Bernie

Although most of the times I play I am aware of the mission I am on, there are times when I just play in a general area on a hospital floor or in the Intensive Care Units.

On one occasion, I played outside a room where I noticed that there was a conference of several doctors with family members. I didn't know what it was about, but the conference broke up quickly. As the doctors came out of the room, some of them gave me a curious glance. I didn't make much of it.

Then family members left the room. Each of them smiled at me. I breathed a prayer of gratitude that the music seemed to help.

One year later, I received a call from Ruth, who wanted me to play for her husband's funeral. She explained to me that I had played for him before, but that I probably didn't realize it. She told me that it was her husband who was the patient in the room with the consulting doctors. He had contracted Legionnaire's Disease and was in an irreversible coma. The doctors were in the room to suggest that Bernie be taken off life support.

As I began playing outside the room, Bernie opened his eyes for the first time in months and began to revive. The doctors cannot explain the reversal of his condition.

Make me a channel of your peace.
Where there's despair in life, let me bring hope.
Where there is darkness, only light, and where there is sadness, joy.
From Prayer of St. Francis

Awake

my Soul.

My heart is steadfast,

God, my heart is steadfast.

I will sing and chant praise.

Awake, my soul; awake, lyre and harp!

I will wake the dawn.

I will praise you among the peoples, Lord;

I will chant your praise among the nations.

For your love towers to the heavens;

your faithfulness, to the skies.

Show yourself over the heavens, God;

may *your glory* appear above all the earth.

Elizabeth and Dorothy

I have several CDs recorded. The marketing of these CDs is done through my religious community via an administrative assistant. The first person who served my ministry in this way was Elizabeth.

One day, Elizabeth was called to the information desk where she found a young woman who wanted to buy another CD. Her next statement came as a complete surprise.

"My name is Dorothy. The music I heard on Sister Malinda's first CD saved me from suicide. I would love to have another one, if there are some different ones."

Elizabeth told me about this young woman with tears in her eyes.

Lord of all gentleness, Lord of all calm,
whose voice is contentment,
whose presence is balm:
be there at our sleeping,
and give us we pray,
your peace in our hearts,
Lord, at the end of the day.

--Irish folk tune

The Harp
A
SYMBOL
of
DIVINE
PEACE

CHTA

Like a child rests in its mother's arms,
  so will I rest in you.
LORD, my heart is not proud;
        nor are my eyes haughty.
I do not busy myself with great matters,
  with things too sublime for me.
Rather, I have stilled my soul,
        hushed it like a weaned child.
Like a weaned child on its
  mother's lap, so is my soul
        within me.
Israel, hope in the LORD,
  now and forever.

Psalm 131

The Triplets

All three babies were in one incubator. I had never seen any babies so tiny in my life. There were tubes and lines connected in various ways to every baby. They were thrashing about, obviously not sleeping. The nurse in the neo-natal unit looked relieved that I was there and indicated where the harp should be located. Then she quietly told me about the set of premature triplets in her care.

I started to play very softly and soon was absorbed in what I was doing. After a little while, the nurse came and sat by my side. Suddenly an alarm sounded, but it stopped almost immediately. The nurse breathed a sigh of relief.

I smiled at her, and kept on playing. After about ten minutes, I noticed that the fidgeting in the incubator had nearly stopped.

The alarm sounded again. This time the nurse went to the control panel and turned off a switch. All was quiet again.

I continued to play for about twenty minutes. Since I was scheduled for another floor in the hospital, I started to leave. The nurse followed me.

"Do you realize that you were a true blessing today?" she said. "The alarms were going off constantly before you came! I was so concerned."

"What do the alarms mean?" I asked.

"Well, maybe one of the babies has stopped breathing, or someone's heart has stopped. It always is something very serious," was the

27

surprising answer.

The soothing properties of the harp seemed to affect the life processes even of these very small people.

Jesus loves the little children,
red and yellow, black and white.
All are precious in His sight!
C. Herbert Woolston, George F. Root

We are
HARPS
that the Angels
Play

Shout for joy to God, all the earth;

sing the glory of His name;

give to him glorious praise!

Psalm 66:1-2

The Harp

A Symbol of disarmament, calming anger with its' GENTLE VOICE

Lord, make me an *instrument* of your compassion.
Prayer of St. Francis
(adapted)

CALLIGRAPHY - CUTA
TEXT - TAYLOR & CRAIN

30

An Instrument of Peace

Carol and Alice

One day, as I was getting the harp from the closet in the hospital chapel, I noticed a woman weeping quietly. I said a prayer for her and went on my way to the ICU.

Before I could set up in the corridor outside the sick rooms, a nurse asked me to go to Room 10. "Alice is very restless. We cannot give her any more medicine now. We have reached her limit. Maybe the harp can relax her. She hasn't slept for days."

As I came into the room, I noticed the woman who had been in the chapel sitting in the corner. She was weeping. The nurse mouthed, "Alice's daughter, Carol."

Alice was moving restlessly in bed, obviously uncomfortable. I breathed a prayer, "Please help me, God. I don't know how to do this." I began to play softly. In about five minutes, I heard the deep, steady breathing of sleep. "Thank you, God," was my silent prayer.

I glanced over at the daughter. Tears were streaming down her cheeks. I smiled and said softly, "We have comforted your mother; now let's see what we can do for her daughter."

I don't know why I used the plural - other than that I am so convinced that God works through us, even in the most common circumstances. I continued to play softly until Carol was calm, and then I quietly left. How very compassionate our God is.

Sleep, my love, and peace attend thee all through the night.
Guardian angels God will send thee all through the night.
Soft the drowsy hours are creeping,
hill and vale in slumber sleeping.
Love alone his watch is keeping, all through the night.

Traditional Welsh ballad

How can we sing a song to

the Lord in a foreign land?
May I never be able

to play the harp again
if I forget you, *Jerusalem*!
May I never be able

to sing again if I do not

remember you,
if I do not think of you as my

greatest *joy*!

Psalm 137

the
Divine
healing
music
of
Hope

Doctor Tom

There must have been something terribly wrong on the third floor of the hospital that fall day. Groups of doctors and nurses were in consultation in every corridor. I could see them in earnest conversation from my central position by the nurses' desk. It was so noisy that I thought my playing would never be heard, much less be of any help.

I began to play the most soothing music I could think of. Slowly the level of chatter diminished. One of the doctors came up to me. "We really needed you here today," he said. I read "Doctor Tom" on his name tag. He rushed off to help another patient.

That day, about six nurses or doctors made comments of gratitude for the calming effects of the harp music.

Dona nobis pacem.
(Lord, give us peace)
Traditional round

Awake, O my soul; awake, *lyre and harp;*
I will wake the dawn.
I will *give thanks* to you among the peoples,
O Lord;
I will chant your praise among the nations,
for your kindness towers to the heavens
and your faithfulness to the skies.

Psalm 58:9-11

Awake
my
Soul.

I will
wake
the Dawn
of
Comfort
Joy and
Love.

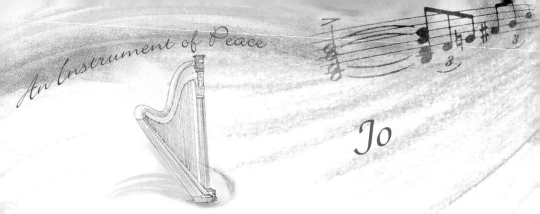

Jo

One of the first places which invited me to play was the renal dialysis unit of a regional hospital where I was to play for the patients while they were getting their treatment. Jo, one of the nurses, said she believed the harp helped them to relax and made the long procedure more bearable.

One day when I arrived, something must have happened which was very stressful for the staff. The noise level was unusually high and people were rushing about frantically. Jo met me and said, "I think you will be needed more for the staff than for the patients today."

I nodded and thought to myself, "I wonder if God and I can help them calm down a bit." I began to play. In a short time the unit was back to its usual serene state, and the nurses were coming to me one by one with gratitude in their eyes and in their voices.

I need Thee ev'ry hour;
Ev'ry hour, I need Thee.
Robert Lowrey

Our LIVES can be Sweet Songs that Melt Fear.

Consolation

As the deer longs for flowing streams,

so longs my soul for you, O God.

My soul does thirst for the living God,

when shall I come to see your face?

Psalm 42

Helen

Although I have played for many people, I have played for only one person during her entire journey through cancer, rehabilitation, recurrence, hospitalization and death. This woman's name was Helen. I came to know her family quite well, so I asked her daughter, Jan, to write the story of Helen's final months. Below is the touching story:

My mom has always liked harp music but rarely had the opportunity to hear it. So the first time we walked into the Cancer Center waiting room and she heard harp music, her face lit up. It surely made the half-hour wait to see her doctor enjoyable. We had the opportunity to be blessed by your music often since we spent many hours in the Cancer Center.

After about a year and a half, Mom's leukemia wasn't responding to any treatments and she became weaker and sicker. At the end of September Mom was moved into my home so I could take care of her. Since I knew she liked harp music I tried to play a CD I had with harp music, but it wouldn't work in the three different boom boxes we have. I felt badly that she couldn't listen to her favorite harp music while confined to bed. Then, three days after her 80th birthday, she was admitted into the hospital. That first day, the chaplain came to visit and prayed with Mom. He asked if she would like to listen to some music. She was happy at that suggestion. I could hardly believe it when he brought in a CD of hymns played on a harp. I remembered how hard I had tried to play the CD of harp music for her at home.

Everyone, including Mom, knew she was dying and just having this music playing made the atmosphere one of peace. At times you could hear her singing along softly on some of her favorite hymns.

When the chaplain heard how Mom loved your music while at the Cancer Center, he arranged for you to come and play in her hospital room.

She grew weaker and sicker as the week wore on. The pain grew so severe she would moan much of the time and at times, thrash around. The first time you came was Thursday. You couldn't find the harp at the hospital so you got the one out of your car. While you played some of her favorite hymns she would stop moaning in pain and even try to mouth the words. You couldn't stay long; you were late for a perform-ance at a nursing home.

To our amazement, you came back the next day. Once again you played and calmness came over my mom. She stopped moaning and tried to sing "Amazing Grace" with you.

My brother asked if you would play at her funeral. You said you would if it worked into your schedule.

We continued to play the harp CD for her after you left. Mom passed away that night and I like to think she is still hearing harp music since she loved it so.

It did work out for you to play for Mom one last time at her funeral. I know she had to be looking down from heaven, smiling. What a blessing you were, not only to my mom but to her family, too.

God bless,
Jan

Lead kindly light, amid the encircling gloom,
lead Thou me on.
The night is dark, and I am far from home,
lead Thou me on.

Keep Thou my feet, I do not ask to see.
Only one step, one little step is all I ask;
one step enough for me.

John Newman

Your love is better than life;

    my speech is full of praise.

I give you a lifetime of worship;

    my hands lifted in prayer.

You have been my help;

    I rejoice beneath your wings.

Selected from Psalm 63

Julie and Lillie

There are many times that the effects of the sounds of the harp are not evident while I am playing.

The benefits derived are far-reaching and are enhanced by recorded music. The following is a testimonial I received from Lynda, Julie's sister:

Back in the winter of 2005-2006 I bought one of your wonderful CDs, Music of Healing Comfort, while accompanying my sister, Julie, to her chemotherapy treatment at Franciscan Skemp. I wanted to give it to her, but she insisted that I keep it and she borrowed it for her use. On March 1, 2006, she learned her chemo was no longer helping her and she had only 2-3 months to live. I brought the CD back to her house and when she passed away on March 29, 2008, her husband was playing it for her. "Amazing Grace" was playing when she took her last breath.

You were playing your harp in the hospital again when my Grandma, Lillie, was there and she passed away at 104 years. I want to thank you so much for your wonderful ministry. Your music was comfort to my sister and still is today to me and to all who listen to it. I've been meaning to send you this thank you for a long time and am now finally getting to it. Thanks again for all you do for everyone. God's blessings on you.

-- Lynda
Galesville, Wisconsin

When we've been there ten thousand years, bright shining as the sun,
we've no less days to sing God's praise than when we first begun.

From "Amazing Grace" by John Newton

O Master, grant that I may not seek

so much to be consoled, as to console...

for it is in dying that we are born

to eternal life.

Prayer of St. Francis

Alfred

My brother Alfred was diagnosed with a non-malignant tumor on his brain in the mid-1990s. Since there were no ill effects from this tumor, his doctors decided to delay treatment until that became necessary. At Christmastime, 2003, Alfred began finding it hard to walk and showed other indications that things were not right. Examinations and tests revealed that the tumor was growing. Further tests revealed that it was cancerous. He underwent nine surgeries between January and mid-October.

When the doctors said they could do no more for him, he decided to leave the hospital and be at home to die. He was given hospice aid. His wife, Ann, two daughters, Connie and Brenda, and son, Derrick, were constantly at his side.

I played for Al several times while he was in the hospital and, also, when he was at home. When I played at his home I used the Irish folk harp that I had purchased with money from a trust fund set up by our mother, who died in 1999. I considered the harp a gift from Mother and hoped she would have approved of my harp ministry. On one occasion while I was playing for Al at home, I started the song "On Eagle's Wings." His face lit up. He remarked, "That song was one we sang at our high school graduation. I really like that song!" Al's son, Derrick, began to take a video of me playing the song so Al could hear it when I was not there. As I was playing, I looked up and saw Al looking at something over my shoulder.

"What is it, Al?" I asked.

"Do you feel that hand on your shoulder?"

Meanwhile, Derrick was concerned that the video camera had stopped working.

"What are you talking about? I don't feel anything," I said. All the while, I continued to play "On Eagle's Wings."

"Well, Mom is standing right behind you with her hand on your shoulder!" Al said.

I continued to play. I realized that I was playing the song by heart. I did not know it from memory then, nor do I now! Mother was coming for Al, and she approved of my work with the harp!

Al continued to talk about Mother for a few minutes. When he stopped talking about her, the video camera started again without any help from Derrick!

Al died peacefully two days later.

Truly, the veil gets thinner as we near death.

And He will raise you up on eagle's wings,

bear you on the breath of dawn,

make you to shine like the sun,

and hold you in the palm of his hand.

From "On Eagle's Wings" by Michael Joncas

He who
bends
to himself
a
joy
of
Goodness lives in
Eternity's
sunRise

Where there is despair

in life,

let me bring hope;

where there is darkness,

light

and where there is sadness,

joy.

Prayer of St. Francis

Margaret

"Would you please come into Margaret's room? She has severe brain damage, and her family has decided to remove her life-support systems."

The nurse in the ICU was concerned and thought that the music of the harp would help in this very difficult situation. I moved into the sick room and started to play softly as the family said their goodbyes. I started to play "How Great Thou Art." The eldest daughter moved to her mother's bedside and began to sing softly into her mother's ear. The only sounds in the room were those of the machines, the harp and the daughter's loving song.

Soon the doctors came in. The family stayed by the bedside as the instruments were carefully removed. At their invitation I continued to play. After the doctors left, the nurses left the monitors on for a few minutes to note lung and heart movements. I paced my playing to the slowing sounds and sights of the monitors. Then the nurse turned off the monitors and I was faced with "Now what do I do?"

"God, please help me to know when to stop," was my silent prayer. I continued to play softly, slowing my pace and my volume. In a few minutes I felt that I should stop. When I did, Margaret took her last breath.

Her husband and children were comforted that their loved one was led into the heavenly embrace in such a soothing manner.

When Christ shall come with shout

of acclamation and take me home,

what joy shall fill my heart!

Then I shall bow in humble adoration,

and there proclaim,

my God, how great thou art!

Then sings my soul, my Savior God to thee,

"How great thou art, how great Thou art!"

From "How Great Thou Art"

by Stuart Hine

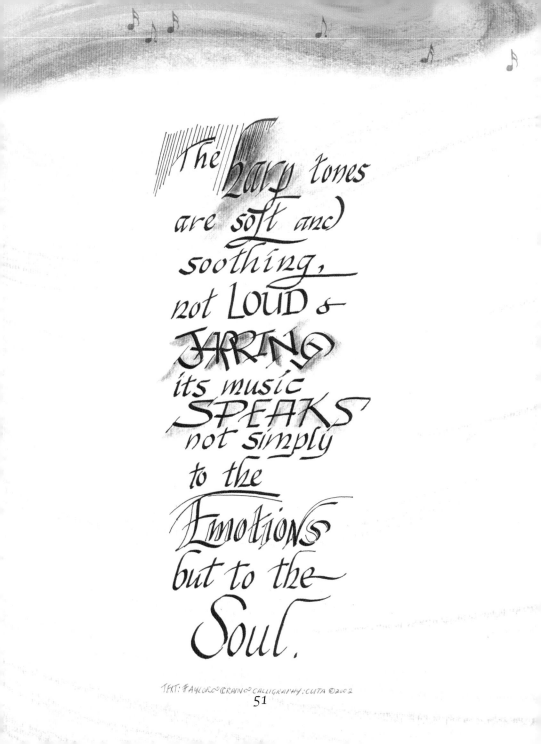

The harp tones are soft and soothing, not LOUD & JARRING its music SPEAKS not simply to the Emotions but to the Soul.

TEXT: TAYLOR CRAIN CALLIGRAPHY: CUTA ©2002

Comfort

But I said, "The LORD has forsaken me;
my Lord has forgotten me."
Can a mother forget her infant, be without
tenderness for the child of her womb?
Even should she forget,
I will never forget you.
See, upon the palms of my hands I have
written your name;
your concerns are ever before me.

Isaiah 49: 14-16 (paraphrased)

Annabelle

I found Annabelle lying on her side with her eyes closed. She might have been sleeping. I had been told that she had recently been diagnosed with a terminal illness. Maybe she just didn't want anything to do with the whole world or anyone or anything in it!

"This could be a challenge," I thought. "Please, God, help me," I prayed.

I began with a few "warm-up" notes, the melody of a familiar setting of St. Francis of Assisi's "Canticle of the Sun." The inspiration for other uplifting hymns followed. I glanced up and noticed Annabelle gazing with half-closed eyes out the window. She didn't move, nor did she acknowledge me.

I smiled to myself. "It's working," I thought.

The next song I thought of was "Simple Gifts." Some people know this melody as "The Lord of the Dance."

'Tis a gift to be simple, 'tis a gift to be free …

Annabelle moved slowly to sit on the edge of the bed. She didn't look at me, but I noticed her foot moving ever so slightly in time with the music.

"Thank you, God!" I thought as I continued to play. Annabelle looked at me.

"Hi, there," I said. "You have such beautiful eyes."

She smiled. "I just got news this morning that I have a terminal illness.

I don't think I'm long for this world. It is so hard. My family won't understand and I ..."

Her voice trailed off. I had to answer, but what would I say? The quote from the Bible "You will be given what to say," came true again, as it has so often in my work.

"Everything will be all right," came out of my mouth. "The thing to remember is that we know that anything which comes our way is from a good God, a God who loves all of us. Your family as well as you will be loved by God through everything."

Annabelle was quiet. Then she said, "Do you play for funerals?"

"Yes, I am honored to play for anyone who asks me."

"That would be nice. I think I will be going home tomorrow. You have been such a help."

"Thank you," I said. "You have just made my day a wonderful one." I haven't heard anything more from Annabelle.

Morning has broken like the first morning.
Blackbird has spoken like the first bird.
Praise for the singing! Praise for the morning!
Praise for them springing fresh from the Word!
Mine is the sunlight! Mine is the morning
born of the one light Eden saw play!
Praise with elation, praise ev'ry morning,
God's re-creation of the new day!
From "Morning Has Broken" by Eleanor Farjeon

So I look to you in the sanctuary
to see your power and glory.
For your love is better than life;
my lips offer you worship!
I will bless you as long as I live;
I will lift up my hands, calling on your name.
My soul shall savor the rich banquet of praise,
with joyous lips my mouth shall honor you!
When I think of you upon
my bed, through the night
watches I will recall
That you indeed are my help,
and in the shadow
of your wings I shout for joy.
My soul clings fast to you;
your right hand upholds me.

Psalm 63:3-9

Rosemary

"I don't think you remember my family," said a distinguished looking man. I had just finished playing for a wedding. Joining the man, who said his name was Tom, was a frail, smiling woman. Tom introduced her as his wife, Rosemary. Two other women, his daughter and granddaughter, were standing close by.

"No, I'm sorry, I don't remember," I said.

Tom explained, "You played for Rosemary when she was in the ICU in the hospital. She was there for over a month, and you came several times to play in her room."

Then Rosemary spoke up. "The only thing I can remember from the hospital is the beautiful sound of the harp as you were playing. I don't remember my husband being there, or my daughter or granddaughter, only you playing the harp."

"Thank you for telling me. I am so happy I could be of help."

Rosemary is almost fully recovered from her illness, and she and her family are convinced of the healing power of the harp.

God is so good,
God is so good,
God is so good, so good to me.
Traditional African melody

Let the children come to me
and do not stop them.
It is to just such as these that
the kingdom of Heaven belongs.

Mark 10:14

Baby Cristofer and Sam

As I entered the neo-natal unit, I heard a pain-filled cry. I prayed, "Lord, make me an instrument of your comforting presence."

I set up the harp. Cristofer, a baby, was protesting to everything the nurse was trying to do to alleviate his pain. I started to play softly and slowly. The crying stopped.

I suggested that the nurse place Cristofer on the floor next to the harp. The nurse placed him in a small carrier equipped with monitor lines. She put the carrier on a blanket on the floor next to me. Only small sounds came from the carrier. I glanced at Cristofer when I heard contented gurgling sounds. He was smiling while he investigated his big toe. The nurse told me that he was born with a bowel that was too short. I shuddered at the thought of how much pain that could cause.

I played there for about a half hour. Although the baby did not sleep, he also did not cry. I could see his contented face and knew that my prayer was answered.

Cristofer was a long-term patient in the unit. He was there the next week when I came to play. This time his father was with him. Cristofer's older brother, Sam, was never far away. Sam was an energetic youngster about three years old. He was not content to sit quietly. There were too many things to explore. Sam became interested in the unit computer, so a nurse placed him on a stool and showed him the keyboard.

Meanwhile, I was playing softly while watching Sam who was trying to entertain himself. I was not surprised when Sam lost interest in the computer. He turned to watch me play. I was surprised when this little boy sat transfixed for a full ten minutes. He just watched and listened. His father and the nurse gave me a smile of gratitude, and I prayed a short prayer of thanksgiving to our understanding God.

Jesus loves the little children, all the children of the world.

From "Jesus Loves the Little Children" by George F. Root

Let's Play the DIVINE MUSIC of Hope to LIGHT UP OUR LIVES.

Music gives a soul to the universe, wings to the mind, flight to the imagination, a charm to sadness, gaiety and life to everything. It is the essence of order and leads to all that is just and good and beautiful.

--Aristotle

After that you will come to Gibeath-Elohim,

where there is a garrison of the Philistines.

As you enter that city, you will meet a band of

prophets, in a prophetic state, coming down from

the high place preceded by

lyres, tambourines, flutes and harps.

The spirit of the Lord will rush upon you,

and you will join them in their prophetic state

and will be changed into another man.

When you see these signs fulfilled,

do whatever you judge feasible, because

God is with you.

I Samuel 10:5-7

Pastor Barbara

Many of the stories of my ministry are about events that occur away from live performances. This is a letter sent to me from a former chaplain who worked in one of the hospitals I serve.

"I've been wanting to let you know how much influence your CDs have had. We bought two sets for the nursing home here in Northwood, and have played them at various times, including during the dying process for some of our residents. I took one when I visited a parishioner who was dying at hospice, and the family played it all night. They were so grateful and said how much it helped them all through the night. They were playing the Healing Comfort CD. I also loaned one to a woman whose husband has a rare brain disease and who (he) has trouble sleeping through the night. She said it helped a lot, and she ordered one for him. In fact, we're getting ready for Bible study here at the home in a few minutes, and the activity director just put one of the CDs in to play. It has helped, and continues to help, so many people."

Blessings always!
Pastor Barbara

Did you ever know that you're my hero,
and ev'rything I would like to be?
I can fly higher than an eagle
'cause you are the wind beneath my wings.
From "Wind Beneath My Wings"
by Larry Henley and Jeff Silbar

65

God, you have taught me from my youth;

to this day I proclaim your **wondrous deeds**.

Now that I am old and gray, do not forsake me, God,

that I **may proclaim** your might

to all generations yet to come.

Psalm 71:18

Josephine and Judith

Often I am asked to play for people with Alzheimer's disease. One of these places is Villa St. Joseph, the retirement home for the sisters of my religious community. I usually play in the terrace, a sunny room with nearly ceiling-to-floor windows which look out on a patio where bird feeders and colorful landscaping invite birds of every color and song. The sisters come to this room to enjoy each other and to be close to nature.

One day as I was playing, I heard Sister Josephine, who was in the advanced stages of dementia, begin to "teach" her "class" arithmetic. "Two and two are four! Don't forget now, this is important!" The class continued for several minutes. Then I heard, "Shhh. Now be quiet and listen to the beautiful music!" Sister Josephine sat still with her hands in her lap and eyes closed as the sounds of the harp quieted her restless spirit.

Sister Judith came into the terrace. She could no longer walk, so a nurse was pushing her in her wheel chair. I could hear her mumbling incoherent sounds. She was rocking back and forth in her chair. I remembered that she, since she was about as Irish as St. Patrick, loved "Morning Has Broken." She called it her "blackbird" song. I began the familiar melody. The mumbling became softer and softer, the rocking, slower and slower. Soon Sister Judith was quiet, a lovely smile on her

67

face. She was listening to her "blackbird" song while enjoying the birds who were singing along with the harp.

He speaks, and the sound of His voice
Is so sweet, the birds hush their singing,
And the melody that He gave to me,
Within my heart is ringing.
And He walks with me, and He talks with me,
And He tells me I am His own;
And the joy we share, as we tarry there,
None other has ever known.

from "In the Garden"
by Austin Miles

May the words of my mouth
and the meditation of my heart
be pleasing in your sight, O Lord,
my Rock and my Redeemer.

Psalm 19:1-4

The Harp
is an
Instrument
of
DIVINE
Music

Nature

I heard
the
Sound
of
Harpists.
A
new hymn
of
praise
&
peace.

72

Susie

"I hope you won't be insulted by this." The head nurse in the neo-natal unit of the hospital looked at me with a slight smile on her face and a twinkle in her eye.

"Why should I?"

"Well, you see, I'm going to tell you what I did for my dog, Susie. Susie was very sick. She was restless and uncomfortable. I thought that she might be helped by listening to your CD, and I was right. The music comforted her so much that she was able to go to sleep, and eventually she got better. That was last summer. Earlier this year, Susie got sick again. This time, the vet told me that Susie was not going to recover. I put the CD on again, and with the same results. Susie died quietly, while listening to the comforting sounds of your harp playing."

"I could never be insulted by a story like that. I am a Franciscan, and I am sure St. Francis could only be pleased," was my response. That day, I learned about the compassion of our God who cares not only for us, but also for the animal members of creation.

Praise God from whom all blessings flow;
praise him, all creatures here below.
From "Doxology" by Thomas Ken

All you beasts, wild and tame,

bless the Lord;

praise and exalt him above all

forever.

Daniel 3:81

Tisha

Tisha is a Siberian Husky. She is a beloved pet who developed a tumor on her left foreleg. The vet performed surgery on the leg. Quite a large amount of tissue and muscle was removed in order to assure complete removal of the tumor.

The night after surgery Tisha's owners took her home. During the night, the Husky became very restless. It looked bad at the time. Danny, the husband of the family, went away on a trucking assignment, so Julie was left alone to tend to the dog. Julie knelt over Tisha who was on a blanket in front of the fireplace. She prayed to God to help her take care of Tisha and to bless her.

The whole family had learned to love and treasure the dog who had been part of their home for eight years. Nothing was helping Tisha to lie quietly until Julie remembered the CD I had given them. The beautiful harp music filled the room. It was helping Tisha and it was helping Julie,

who was afraid and tired and worried. She wrote me a letter that the music did wonders for them. Now Tisha is up with a bounce in her step, a friendly wave in her tail, and the sparkle is back in her eyes.

O God, almighty Father,
Creator of all things,
The heavens stand in wonder,
while earth your glory sings.
From "O God, Almighty Father"
by Irvin Udulutch

75

An Instrument of Divine Music

About the Author

Sister Malinda Gerke is a member of the Franciscan Sisters of Perpetual Adoration. She is a native of La Crosse, Wisconsin, and currently residing there. Sister Malinda earned a Bachelor's degree in Music Education from Viterbo University, La Crosse, Wisconsin, a Master's degree in Music Education from the University of Wisconsin-Milwaukee, and a Master's certificate in Liturgy from Notre Dame University, Notre Dame, Indiana.

Most of Sister Malinda's professional career was spent as a teacher of private instrumental music, and elementary and high school choral music. In 1990, she was appointed as liturgy co-ordinator of St. Rose Convent, the Motherhouse of the Franciscan Sisters of Perpetual Adoration.

During Sister Malinda's term as liturgy co-ordinator at St. Rose, she located the antique classic harp which was among the community's treasures for a long time. It was in need of major repair. At Sister Malinda's request, the decision was made to rebuild the harp in 1997. That was when Sister Malinda began to learn to play the harp. Her goal was to give voice to this beautiful instrument. She retired in 2001, and has since developed her passion for playing the harp. She works as a volunteer in the local hospitals and in some of the nursing homes and assisted living residences in the area. She also plays for religious functions at St. Rose and at local churches. Funerals and weddings are part of her schedule. Sister Malinda has produced five CDs in addition to this book, *Instrument of Peace*.

Although she has had no formal training as a harp therapist, or as a music therapy practitioner, her work has brought comfort and peace to all who have heard her play.

The Companion CD to Instrument of Peace

The CD included in the book *Instrument of Peace* is a collection of pieces portraying the various aspects of experiences spoken of in the book. Some of them are the actual music used, while some are pieces which invite the same emotional responses as those used in the actual situations.

1. "Amazing Grace" traditional   01:43
2. "The Search" by Sister Malinda Gerke   02:40
3. "Precious Lord" traditional   01:31
4. "Sinfoni" from Contata No. 156 by Bach   04:45
5. "Lord of all Hopefulness" traditional Irish melody   01:35
6. "Dona Nobis Pacem" traditional   02:45
7. "Prayer of Peace" by Sister Barbara Freed, FSPA   02:40
8. "Prelude in C" by Bach   02:27
9. "Remember Me" by Thomas Haweis, arr. Pam Ohms
10. "The Water is Wide" traditional Irish melody   02:40
11. "Pavane Our Une Infante Defunte" by Maurice Ravel   02:43
12. "Jesu, Joy of Man's Desiring" by J.S. Bach   02:59
13. "Star of the County Down" traditional Irish melody   02:19
14. "Sheebeg and Sheemore" traditional Irish melody   02:22
15. "Dreams of Spring" by Karl Weinand   04:10
    (Deer Hollow Publication)
16. "Wild Mountain" traditional Irish melody   01:48
17. "Greensleeves" traditional English melody   02:08
18. "How Great Thou Art" by Stuart K. Hine   03:21
19. "Canon in D" by Johann Pachelbel   04:01
                                        Total Time   52:03

All musical numbers arranged for harp by Sister Malinda Gerke
unless otherwise indicated.

CD Mechanical License
"Dreams of Spring" by Karl Wienand published by Deer Hollow Publications.
License procured.
Website: www.deerhollow.com

Quantity	Product	Price	Total
	Emmanuel (Christmas) CD	$15.00	
	Emmanuel (Christmas) Cassette	$10.00	
	Healing Comfort CD	$15.00	
	Healing Comfort Cassette	$10.00	
	Prayerful Impressions CD	$15.00	
	Prayerful Impressions Cassette	$10.00	
	Peaceful Journey CD	$15.00	
	Peaceful Journey Cassette	$10.00	
	Reflection and Praise CD	$15.00	
	Reflection and Praise Cassette	$10.00	
	Instrument of Peace Book w/CD	$22.95	
	Sub Total		

Postage charges for mailed orders will be added to final total.
You may also order on line at www.ruahmedia.org.

Ship to:

Name _____

Address _____

City _____

State _____ Zip _____

Daytime Phone _____

Credit Card # _____

Exp. Date _____

> **Mail Order to:**
> Franciscan Sisters of
> Perpetual Adoration
> 912 Market Street
> La Crosse, Wisconsin 54601-0242
> *Thank You*
> *Prepare checks payable to Franciscan*
> *Sisters of Perpetual Adoration (FSPA).*

Other Recordings

Prayerful Impressions

Prayerful Impressions is a collection of pieces played on the harp which provides a relaxing and gentle atmosphere for assisting in meditation and prayer or for stress relieving background music. Much of the music is improvised based on the Gregorian Chant Kyries.

Reflection and Praise

Music for Reflection and Praise is a collection of familiar hymns and reflective music arranged for flute, cello and harp. The music is superimposed over recordings of nature sounds from throughout the United States. The recordings of nature were done by nature enthusiast Jeff Cozy. The CD was recorded in the historic chapel of Mary of the Angels at St. Rose Convent in La Crosse, Wisconsin. The harp used is an antique harp built by Lyon and Healy in Chicago.

Emmanuel

This selection of Christmas music arranged for flute, cello and harp was made to celebrate the miracle of "Emmanuel, God with us." Every Christmas season the beloved songs of the season sound again, reminding us of the continual presence of God among us. God manifests himself not only through the historical gift of Jesus becoming one of us, but also by being present to us today as we read the Holy Scriptures and gather to worship in our churches.

Peaceful Journey

Peaceful Journey is an album of harp solos intended for calming the spirit. It is appropriate to use for serious illnesses and hospice work, as well as for general relaxation purposes. Many of the selections are the familiar "comfort" hymns.

Healing Comfort

Music for Healing Comfort was recorded in response to the most frequently requested music at the hospitals and nursing homes. The album is arranged for flute, cello and harp. It contains such beloved melodies as "Danny Boy," "The Rose" and "On Eagle's Wings."

To order any of these recordings, please visit:

www.ruahmedia.org

Thoughts of Peace

_____

_____

_____

_____

_____

_____

_____

_____

_____

_____